Taaniko

Taaniko*

Taaniko is a weaving technique devised by the Maori of New Zealand probably during the 14th or 15th century. Taaniko weaving makes use of twisting movements of the hands and wrists to manipulate fibers into a woven product. Neither tools nor loom are used.

Taniko is the early spelling. During the 1960s the University of Auckland's Department of Anthropology devised a new spelling for the Maori language. This resulted in the more recent spelling *taaniko*.

TAANIKO

Maori Hand-Weaving

by Joyce Ronald Smith

Charles Scribner's Sons • New York

First Published in 1975
by Charles Scribner's Sons, New York

Produced by Vineyard Books, Inc.

This book published simultaneously in
the United States of America and in Canada.

Copyright 1975 in all countries of the International Copyright Union by Vineyard Books, Inc. All rights reserved. No
part of this book may be reproduced in any form without
the permission of Charles Scribner's Sons.

1 3 5 7 9 11 13 15 17 19 I/C 20 18 16 14 12 10 8 6 4 2

Printed in Hong Kong

Library of Congress Catalog Card Number 74-24821

ISBN 0-684-14204-X

Quotations from *The Art of Taaniko Weaving* by S.M. Mead
are used with permission of A.H. & A.W. Reed

Acknowledgments

I am grateful to the following for their assistance in the preparation of this book:

Peter Fetchko, Peabody Museum, Salem, Mass.; Hugo Leckey; Peter Peryer; Morgan Rockhill; Mark Sexton; Tracy Thurber; William Wagner; Color Lab, Providence, R.I.; Field Museum of Natural History, Chicago, Illinois; New Zealand Consulate, New York City; all of my students whose work appears in this book.

Special gratitude goes to Richard Lawton who edited and designed *Taaniko*.

Photograph credits: New Zealand Consulate – 12, 22, 28, 30; H. Lane Smith – 15, 49; Morgan Rockhill – 17, 20, 74, 77, 80-81, 83; Peter Peryer – 24; William Wagner – 18 (bottom); Mark Sexton – 32, 40, 48, 68, 87; Tracy Thurber – 35-39, 42-47, 50-54, 58 (right), 59, 62-64, 69-73, 75-76, 79, 84-85.

for Lane

CONTENTS

Taaniko

INTRODUCTION

I first learned how to do taaniko weaving aboard a ship in the middle of the Pacific Ocean. My husband, Lane, our two children, Adam and Jenny Lane, and I were en route to Auckland, New Zealand. Lane, who is a landscape painter, had arranged for a sabbatical year from teaching, and New Zealand with its natural beauty seemed a perfect spot for painting.

We had brought along many books on New Zealand and some simple art supplies to help pass the many days at sea. One of my books was Sydney M. Mead's *The Art of Taaniko Weaving*. Mr. Mead, a Maori, is an anthropologist who specializes in the field of Maori language and handicrafts. I found myself engrossed in his description of the history and development of taaniko from the time of Captain Cook's first visit to New Zealand in 1769 to the present time.

I was astonished to learn that taaniko, a weaving technique developed by the Maori, required no tool and no loom! And that the weaver is free to introduce as many colors as desired without restriction.

Although Mr. Mead's book is primarily concerned with taaniko weaving in relation to history, social changes, classification of designs, and function for the Maori, it does include an appendix concerning the techniques of taaniko weaving. I quickly devoured the instructions on how to make a taaniko belt.

I rummaged around in a suitcase and found some fine yarn. It wasn't linen as the directions required, but in mid-ocean I would have to substitute. At first the weaving seemed very strange and awkward to my fingers, the only tools needed. However, it soon became a great pleasure. What a technique! I could work outdoors while getting some sun or indoors in the evening. I could do taaniko while sitting down or standing up, and there was no paraphernalia to lug about.

The belt was finished a few days before our arrival in New Zealand. It was beautiful! I wanted to do more and more. I could hardly wait to get more information from the Maori. After all, Mead's book had only told how to make a belt and I wanted to delve much further into the technique.

I felt a little self-conscious wearing my taaniko belt as I went down the gangplank onto New Zealand soil. How presumptuous of me to wear a first project taaniko belt in the land where this weaving method was devised! But I thought my crude effort might be a good conversation piece for me to learn more from the people.

OPPOSITE Maori dancers doing the Canoe Poi Dance. Note the taaniko bodices and headbands on the women and bandoliers on the men.

After going through customs we had to wait on the street for a taxi. No one seemed to notice my belt. And I saw no one else wearing taaniko belts. A friendly taxi driver picked us up and took us to our motel. I asked him where I could find examples of taaniko and see people doing it. "What's that," he asked, "one of those new dance steps?"

I explained what taaniko was, and he suggested we visit the Auckland War Memorial Museum. I took his advice and soon found many beautiful Maori cloaks with taaniko borders, taaniko bodices, headbands and bandoliers. The complexity of these taaniko products fascinated me. The cloaks included feathers and bits of fur for added warmth.

After several days in Auckland, we decided to drive north. We headed toward the part of New Zealand where Captain Cook landed, where the earliest white settlements were, and where a large percentage of the Maori still live. We hoped to settle in a village where Lane could paint, the children could go to school, and I could learn more about taaniko.

After ten days of exploring, we found the perfect village, an incredibly beautiful spot. Russell is the name of the village and it is situated at the end of a long peninsula which juts out into the Bay of Islands. We found an adobe cottage and studio on a lovely beach over the hill from the center of Russell. The children quickly made friends and loved going to the local school where they were urged not to wear shoes.

Russell is a village of about 800 people, both Maori and Pakeha (a Maori word for non-Maoris and used commonly by all). People were warm and friendly, and it was easy to make friends by chatting in Miller's General Store near the town wharf, the hub of the village.

Three weeks had gone by without my doing any taaniko or discussing it with anyone. Now we were settled, I could get back to it.

I inquired about taaniko and met several Maori women who had learned it as children in Maori schools, but they had not kept it up. When I asked why, they said that it had been taught using very fine threads and was too tedious for a child to retain interest. Most of the Russell women were very active with their hands, doing spinning, knitting and macrame. But no taaniko!

I decided to plow ahead on my own. Mead had suggested, in his book, that one should use a fine linen fiber for taaniko. Miller's General Store had no linen but they had plenty of wool and so did the local spinners. I started making more belts. I whipped off half a dozen using three and four colors. I used wool for some, jute and cotton cord for others. No matter which fiber I used the results turned out very nicely.

OPPOSITE Our adobe cottage on Long Beach.

Then I decided to try a sampler wall-hanging using all of the combinations of colors, spacing, weaving and fibers that I could imagine. This method of weaving, so ingeniously devised by the Maori, seemed to be begging me to release it from the past, experiment with it, and realize its vast potential.

I made rugs, wall-hangings, lamp shades, jewelry, and many belts. More and more frequent visitors came to our cottage to look at Lane's paintings and my taaniko. And then one day a friend asked if I would consider giving lessons. I thought, why not?

Up went a sign in the butcher shop window announcing classes in taaniko weaving at the adobe cottage on Long Beach.

People came, Maori and Pakeha alike, to learn taaniko. Each person in the classes taught me a new variation in the use of taaniko. They were all able to do it with lovely individual designs and colors, even though none of them had any experience in design or art training.

Later in the year, when we were traveling, I met a few taaniko weavers in Auckland and Rotorua. These women were weaving in the fine way Mead had suggested, carrying on the Maori symbols and colors. However, they did not have a large following and they did not have the spirit of inventiveness which was evident in the Russell weavers.

The breath of taaniko had been reduced to a thin sigh and I was hoping it would wake up with a vigorous deep breath and continue in a new healthy way. But now our time was up; our visas were about to expire, and we had to leave New Zealand.

In three days we were whisked back to Providence, R.I., in the unreality of jet time. We greatly missed the beauty of New Zealand and its people with their combination of ruggedness and gentleness. Lane kept painting New Zealand landscapes and I kept doing taaniko. Now the excitement about it was even more compelling than before. The urgency of renewing a practically lost art kept beckoning me on. I began teaching classes in Rhode Island. As I did more teaching, I devised more diagrams, slides, and written material. Ultimately it seemed that the best way to teach the most people how to do taaniko was to write a book about it. It is an ingenious and beautiful art with great appeal to many, many people.

Tapeka Pt. Russell, Bay of Islands N.Z. Lane Smith 71

Lane's drawing of Tapeka Point on the North Island.

LEFT Our friend John Moffett vigorously weaving his first belt.

OPPOSITE Our Russell neighbor Irma Ellis finishing her first taaniko sampler.

BELOW A series of first project taaniko belts.

19

Whareunga Bay, N.Z.   MonoPrint drawing #46   H. Lane Smith 72

Lane's monoprint of Whareunga Bay.

The influx of Europeans to New Zealand, beginning with the arrival of Captain Cook in 1769, caused drastic changes in Maori life and spiritual beliefs. The importance of taaniko weaving would die with the Maori acceptance of European modes of living and dress. Elsdon Best describes the sadness of this change in *Spiritual and Mental Concepts of the Maori:*

> The life-weary Maori will never again break out the trails of new realms, never again turn his mythopoetic mind to seek the secrets of the universe. For his sacred life-principle is befouled of man; he has lost caste, and there is no health in mind or body. . . . The great ocean world that he explored, and peopled, and traversed for so many centuries will know him never again, and the last of the gallant old path-finders may truly say, *"Tangi kau ana te hau ki runga o Marae-nui o Hine-moana"* ("Nought save the wailing of the wind is heard on the vast plaza of the Ocean Maid").[1]

[1]Best, Elsdon, Dominion Museum Monograph No. 2, *Spiritual and Mental Concepts of the Maori*, R.E. Owen, Government Printer, Wellington, 1954. The quote is from page 57.

HOW DID TAANIKO DEVELOP

*Taaniko is not weaving in the true sense of the word, but rather
a combination of basketry and plaiting.*

According to anthropologists the Maori arrived in New Zealand around 1350 A.D. No one knows from which Polynesian Island they came. It also remains a mystery why the Maori left one island group in favor of another to the west. Perhaps they had experienced a shortage of food or a terrifying war. At any rate they arrived in New Zealand in long canoes, carrying with them seeds to plant and cultivate in the soil of their new home.

The three important seeds which they carried were the kummera, which produced a sweet potato-like plant and was the mainstay of their diet. The second was the pumpkin which also produced food. (After drying, the outer shells of the pumpkin were used as calabashes.) And the third seed produced the paper mulberry tree. In their original home the bark of the paper mulberry tree was used in the making of bark cloth for clothing. It is important to note that weaving was unheard of in tropical climates. No evidence of any looms or true weaving has ever been found in any of the Polynesian Islands.

When the Maori settled in New Zealand they found that the climate was temperate rather than tropical. The kummera and pumpkin plants survived in the new soil but the paper mulberry tree did not prosper. At the time of Captain Cook's arrival in 1769 he observed very few mulberry trees, and today they are extinct in New Zealand.

The failure of the paper mulberry tree to acclimate caused a clothing problem for the Maori. How would they protect their bodies against the rain and temperate chill? Since there were no mammals to provide skins, only birds, fish and plant life were available to provide their clothing needs.

OPPOSITE Maori woman wearing a cloak with taaniko borders and a taaniko headband.

LEFT New Zealand flax plant (*Phormium tenax*).

OPPOSITE Taaniko border on section of a Maori cloak. (Field Museum of Natural History, Chicago, Illinois.)

Basic Materials Used

The New Zealand flax plant (*Phormium tenax*) was a very common sight in all parts of the North Island where the Maori first settled. This plant is not like the European or New England flax which produces linen fibers from its stem. The New Zealand flax plant is a tall (five or six feet), broad, pointed-leaf plant and in this type of flax the leaves, not the stem, produce the linen fibers.

From their experience on other Pacific Islands, the Maori did have a knowledge of plaiting (braiding or pleating) and basketry. Using these techniques with native flax cut into strips, they made mats, receptacles for food, eel traps and fish nets. Here the flax worked very well, but for clothing it was too stiff.

The Maori next devised a way of exposing the soft inner fibers of the leaf of the flax plant by scraping away the outer portion of the leaf with the edge of a mussel shell. These inner fibers were then washed and sun-dried before being spun and plied by a rolling method along the leg and thigh of the weaver. This method of preparing fibers from the flax leaf and the spinning process are explained in detail in Appendix I.

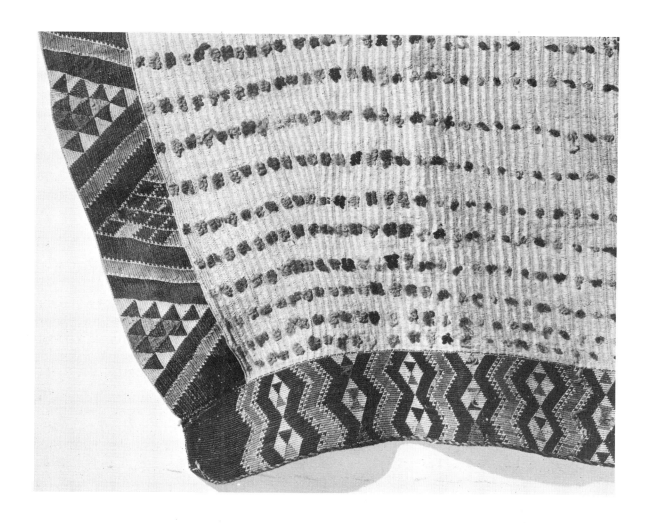

Maori Clothing

With these spun fibers the Maori made loincloths, kilts and cloaks. After the arrival of the English, the bodice was developed for the women and the bandolier for the men.

The cloaks were the largest articles made and it was in these that the finest weaving was done. They were rectangular in shape and were attached at the shoulders. The Maori cleverly wove in gussets at the shoulders and the buttocks to give the cloak a slight shape. The major portion of the cloak was plain but the borders and edges were decorated bands of fine weaving using three and four colors. These are the taaniko portions of the cloaks. (Taaniko also has a more general meaning which refers to all of the weaving techniques in this book.) The borders were tightly woven and were considered too stiff to be next to the skin. The main part of the cloak, the kaupapa, was woven more loosely with the weft rows spaced apart. For additional warmth bird feathers or dog fur were woven into the kaupapa section. This book will be concerned both with taaniko and kaupapa weaving since they are two variations of one weaving technique.

Ornamentation and Color

In their wood carving and hand painting on wood the Maori use curves and arabesques to create designs and symbols. In taaniko weaving, however, the Maori used only diagonal straight lines. As a result all of the designs were based on the triangle, chevron, diamond and pyramid. Perhaps one reason for this is that the knowledge of plaiting that the Maori brought with them to New Zealand was based on a diagonal structure. These designs were like a form of writing to the Maori, who had no written language.

In 1926, Ettie A. Rout wrote a book entitled *Maori Symbolism*, a fascinating account of the sacred legends of the Maori. These legends were handed down from generation to generation by selected members of the Maori nobility through songs and recitations. However, as the young Maori became more and more Europeanized, it became more difficult for the elders to convince the young to memorize the sacred legends.

Miss Rout, a New Zealand lawcourt reporter, took down all of these oral traditions from Chief Hohepa Te Rake. Her observations on Maori art apply equally well to Maori weaving: "When we speak of Maori Art it must be understood that we speak of Maori Symbolism. There was no Art apart from Symbolism – that is, there was no such thing as Art for Art's sake. The carving was not sculpture in the European sense at all: it was writing and expression of ideas and principles. Thus to describe a Maori carving as "crude" is absurd. One might as well describe a printed page as a "crude" picture of insects or birds. The twin ideals of Ancient Maori life were Beauty and Duty, but Beauty must be expressed through the performance of the Duty of cultivation. On this Religion of Cultivation and its Symbolism the whole of Maori Life and Art was based."[2]

S.M. Mead, Te Rangi Hiroa (Sir Peter Buck) and H. Ling Roth have written extensively on the Maori designs and symbols and their classification. A list of their books appears in the bibliography.

The prominent colors used by the Maori in taaniko were red, black and white. Their dye solutions were made from the barks of various New Zealand trees. Appendix II at the end of this book gives a detailed account of how these dyes were made.

[2]Ettie A. Rout, *Maori Symbolism* (London: Harcourt, Brace, 1926).

Drawings of Maori designs used in taaniko borders. (*New Zealand's Heritage*, vol. 2, part 26.)

Oil painting *Maori Women Weaving* by Gottfried Lindauer (1839-1926). (The Auckland City Art Gallery, Auckland, New Zealand.)

Maori Weavers

Only certain women did the weaving in a Maori Pa (settlement), and before a young girl could become a full-fledged weaver she had to go through initiation ritual performed by the priest (tohunga). This is beautifully described by Mead:

As the girl grew up she watched, asked questions, and practiced weaving until the point was reached when she thought she was good enough to be an independent weaver. No modern weaver whom I interviewed was ever trained by a tohunga (priest). Each one learned because she wanted to and in nearly every case was at first discouraged. Not until a mother was convinced of her earnestness would she set out to teach a daughter what she knew.

At this point the tohunga was called in. The tohunga and the weaver seeking initiation into the craft guild, or whare pora, sat alone in the house, the weaver seated before the two weaving pegs. The first weft thread known as taawhiu is tied across the two weaving pegs (turu-turu). The warp threads are doubled over the taawhiu and the weaver is ready to weave the first row of interlocking twines. But before she does so the tohunga recites this spell:

Stick in the peg, it is the peg,
Of eager desire, of swiftness.
Stand medium of authority, stand medium of the house.
Send here the weft to be hastily woven
So it may be woven quickly to be soon completed.
Soon above, soon below;
Soon to be completed the bottom end,
Completed wide apart, completed in the house.
Tremble the hill,
The hill heaped up, the mound gathered together;
Heaped up to the sky,
Widely across the land
Be completed! Be completed!

When the spell is completed the weaver bends forward and bites the sacred peg, which is the right weaving peg. Obviously the sacred peg is the medium and the vehicle by which the effectiveness of the spell enters the weaver's mouth, thence to the stomach. Having received the ritual blessing she weaves the sacred weft.

The rules which the whare pora encouraged weavers to follow were ritualistic rather than technical. They are as follows:

1. Fine garments should be woven only in the daytime.
2. When the sun sets the sacred peg must be taken down, the work rolled up and covered.
3. Cloaks and kilts may be woven at night.
4. Weaving must be done under cover.
5. At the approach of strangers the work must be rolled up and covered.
6. Women should not smoke while weaving.

When the husband of a weaver died the widow lived in the house of mourning (whare tauaa). Here, while under the restrictions that are part of mourning ceremonies, she wove a ritual cloak called kaakahu roimata (cloak of tears). The weaving of this garment was referred to as what tangi (the weaving of lamentation). These cloaks were used to wrap up the bones of the corpse after exhumation.[3]

[3]S.M. Mead, *Traditional Maori Clothing* (Auckland: A.H. & A.W. Reed, 1969).

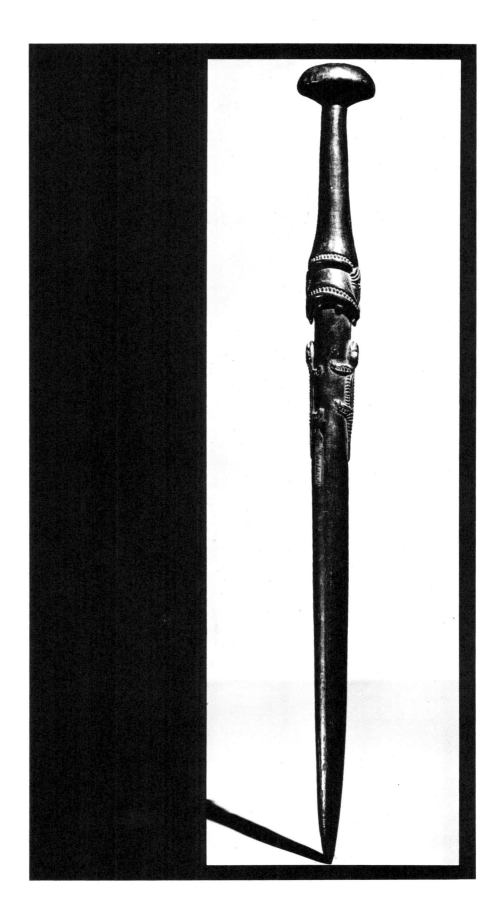

LEFT Maori dancers showing a stick game in progress. Note the taaniko bodices, bandoliers and headbands.

RIGHT Sacred weaving peg. (Field Museum of Natural History, Chicago, Illinois.)

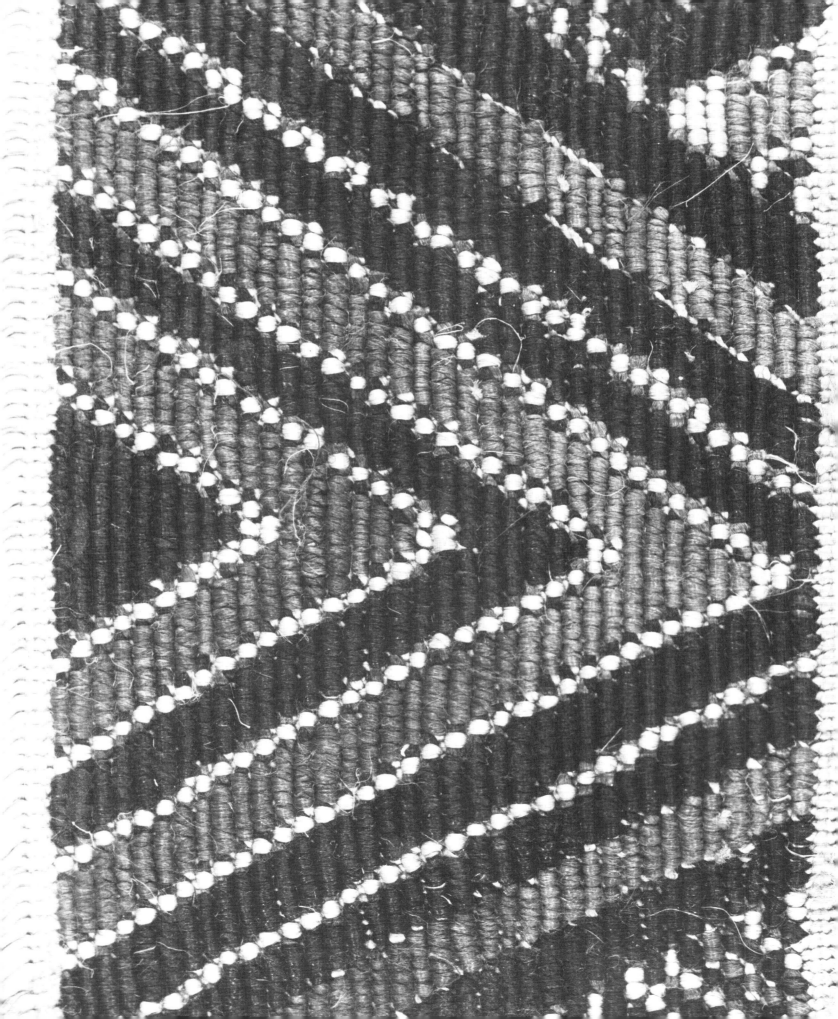

CASTING ON

Stick in the peg; it is the peg,
Of eager desire, of swiftness . . .

This chapter and the following ones will give, in detailed diagrams, photographs and written explanations, the process of taaniko weaving.

Warp refers to the fibers which run up and down or vertically in a piece of weaving.

Weft refers to the fibers which run left to right or horizontally in a piece of weaving.

A Synopsis of the Taaniko Weaving Process

The three parts of taaniko weaving are: casting on, weaving, and casting off.

In **casting on** two pairs of weft fibers are interlocked to connect each warp fiber, one at a time. The warp fibers will hang freely but are attached at the top by the casting on process.

The **weaving** is done with one pair of weft fibers for two colors, three weft fibers for three colors, etc. By a rotation of the wrist the weft fibers are crossed and the warp is placed in between. One rotation of the wrist changes the color of the next stitch and two rotations of the wrist repeats the same color for the next stitch.

In **casting off** the procedure is to fold back the free hanging warps to create a bottom edge to the piece which will look like the top casting on edge. Again two pairs of weft fibers are used which interlock the warps and at the same time fold the warps to the back side of the weaving. Casting off is used mainly in belts and headbands. In things such as rugs, hangings, and hand bags, the warp ends can be trimmed or wrapped with other fibers.

Traditionally taaniko was woven from left to right, the weft fibers being knotted and trimmed at the end of each row. However, in my classes, students and I have devised several ways of weaving back and forth continuously. (This is explained in Chapter V on Variations.) For the beginner it is easier to start the traditional way of one row at a time, going only from left to right. When the fingers and the wrists are familiar with the taaniko process, then the continuous weaving will come easily.

OPPOSITE Enlarged section of taaniko border on a Maori cloak. (Peabody Museum, Salem, Mass.)

As shown in the Lindauer painting (*page 28*) and in the descriptions of the Maori rituals involving taaniko, the women wove between two pegs. When first learning taaniko, I too attempted to suspend the weaving between two upright poles. However, I found it completely unnecessary and actually more comfortable to hold the work in my lap, or, if it involves a large piece, to place the weaving on a table in front of me. Occasionally for large pieces of weaving my students have tried attaching the cast on row to a frame (a simple wooden rectangle or a wooden canvas stretcher frame) and then laying the frame on a table for weaving. These simple frames, or poles as the Maori used, are in no way involved with the actual weaving and cannot be considered looms. Mostly my students and I prefer to work without anything for support.

Beginning Project

As stated earlier, there are three parts to taaniko weaving: casting on, weaving and casting off. In making wall-hangings, purses, rugs, jewelry and lamp shades, generally only casting on and weaving are used. However, all three steps are used when making a belt. This repetition will give the beginner an opportunity to become familiar with the weaving action.

For the first project it is best to use heavy rug yarn for the weft fibers, the part which will show most on the belt. Wool, cotton, cotton blends or synthetics may be used, and rug yarns are available at most dime stores, department stores and yarn shops. In the beginning it is best to use only two colors. Select two contrasting colors which you feel go well together; a two-ounce skein of each color will be more than enough for the belt.

You may use jute, sisel, macrame cord or cotton cable cord for the warp fibers. These are available in hardware stores, dime stores, hobby shops and specialty yarn shops. The warps show only a little on the edges of the belt, but choose a warp color which will go with the two colors you have selected for the weft. Since the belt is your first project, the warp should be a stiffer fiber than the weft fibers, simply because a warp with more body is easier to handle. Actually anything can be used for warp fibers but in the beginning something soft and floppy will be more difficult to work with.

The warp and weft fibers should be approximately the same weight or thickness.

Designing the Belt

To work out your design you will need graph paper and pencil, pens or colored pencils. On the graph paper one square will represent one stitch or one warp. The belt should be at least five rows of weaving wide. If you are using normal rug yarn this will result in a belt approximately 2 inches wide.

Since taaniko is done one stitch at a time, design possibilities are endless. To illustrate how a design can be worked out, at the top of **page 35** is a graph showing five rows of weaving.

Measure the number of inches around your waist or hips, depending on where you will be wearing your belt. The belt should nearly meet in front, leaving room for an added fringe for tying or a buckle. When you have established this measurement, multiply it by *four* and cut two lengths, one of each weft color. Next cut about thirty warps, each *four times* as long as the width of the belt (in this case if the belt is to be two inches wide, the warps will be eight inches long). More warps will be needed as you weave, but these can be cut later.

You are now ready to cast on and for this you can put your design aside. Casting on means connecting all of the warp fibers in a free hanging position. The casting on process takes up the same amount of room as two rows of weaving. Its visual characteristic is a herringbone appearance as shown in the photograph below.

A Note on Diagrams and Photographs

On the following pages the drawn diagrams represent the placement of fibers step by step. Each diagram is accompanied by a photograph which shows how your hands are to hold the fibers. In the photographs hands sometimes unavoidably cover the fiber movements, in which case the eye can travel back to the diagram which will show more clearly how the fibers are placed.

I have used a great many diagrams in order to give a slow-motion presentation for the beginner. The actual weaving is not nearly as difficult as the number of diagrams and photographs might indicate; however, presenting an unfamiliar technique seemed to me to require detailed visual material.

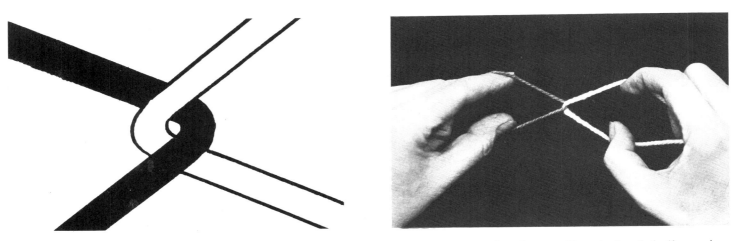

Figure 1 Take the two weft fibers and hook them together at the mid-point of each one. (For clarity I shall say that the two colors are black and white.) You now have a pair of black fibers in the left hand and a pair of white fibers in the right hand.

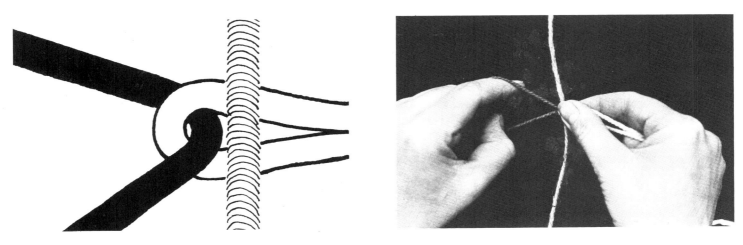

Figure 2 Pick up one of the warp fibers at the mid-point and lay it across the pair of white weft fibers which are being held close together in the right hand. This warp must now be secured in place.

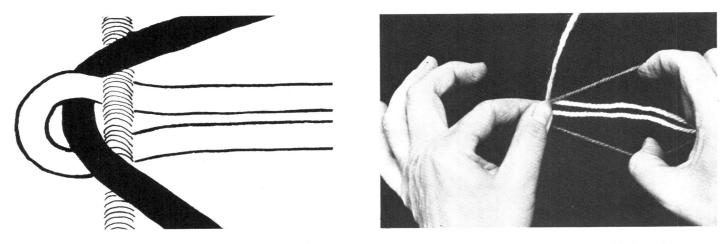

Figure 3 To secure the warp, take the pair of black weft fibers on the left, spread them apart, and bring them over to the right side.

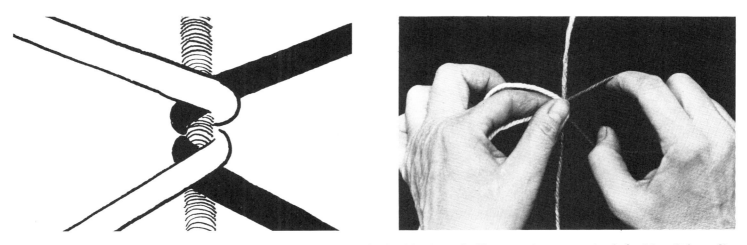

Figure 4 The white weft fibers are now brought through the black weft fibers and over to the left side. (I just flip the weft fibers back and forth, but if they seem awkwardly long, they can be rolled and held loosely with an elastic band.) Of course, as you weave, the weft fibers will get shorter.

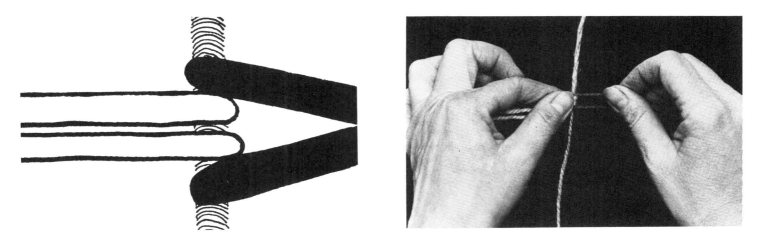

Figure 5 Both black and white weft fibers are pulled tight to secure the first warp.

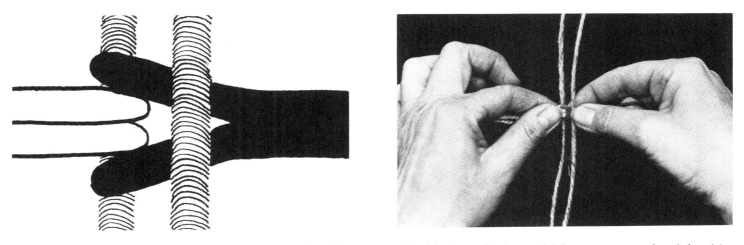

Figure 6 Now lay another warp fiber at its mid-point, across the black weft fibers which are now on the right side.

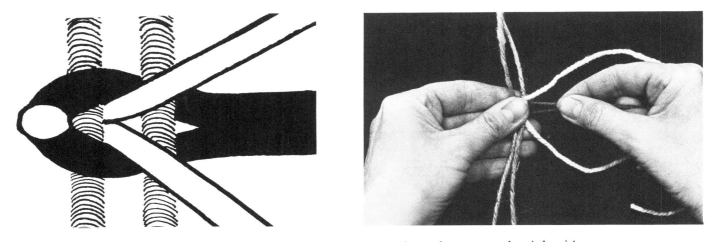

Figure 7 The white weft fibers on the left are now spread apart and brought over to the right side.

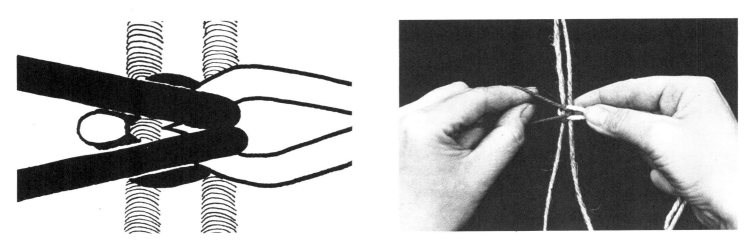

Figure 8 The black weft fibers are brought through the white weft fibers and over to the left side. The second warp is now secured by pulling both black and white weft fibers tight.

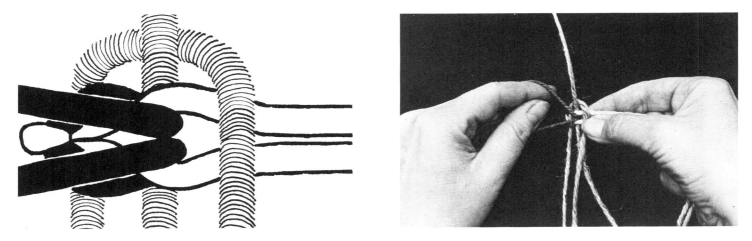

Figure 9 So far you have cast on two warp fibers with two warp ends pointing up and two ends hanging down. Since you want all of the warps to hang down, take the warp end on the left pointing up, bring it in back of the second warp and have it hanging down across the white weft fibers.

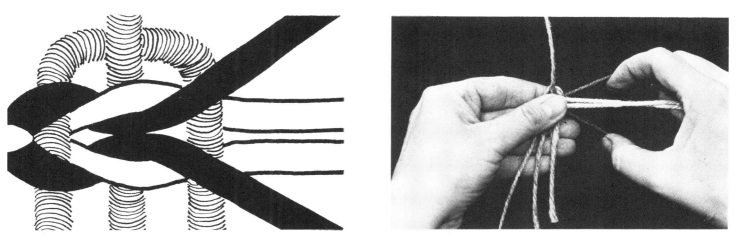

Figure 10   This new warp will be secured as any other warp, by taking the black weft fibers on the left side, spreading them apart and bringing them over to the right side.

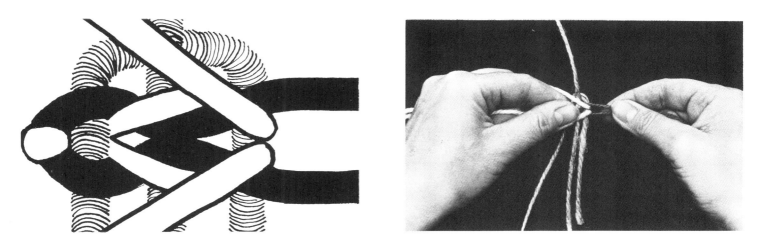

Figure 11   The white weft fibers are now brought through the black weft fibers and over to the left side.

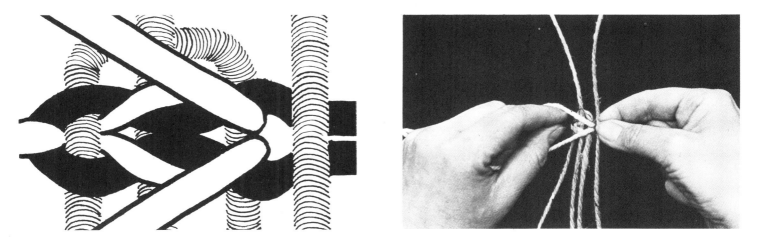

Figure 12   Three warp ends are now hanging down and one warp end is pointing up. Next add a new warp and secure it as you did the first and second warps. Continue the process of bending over warp ends and adding new warps until the desired length of the belt is reached. Finish off the row by tying the black and white weft fibers into a square knot.

WEAVING

Stand medium of authority, stand medium of the house,
Send here the weft to be hastily woven . . .

You now have the belt cast on with all of the free hanging warps pointing down. At this point if you spread the cast on portion of the belt on a table you will notice that on the top edge, where the warps were bent over, the loops will be uneven. Take the work in your hands and give a stout tug on all of the warps, one at a time, pulling each one down through the double row of cast on weft fibers. After this is done the top edge will be much more even. This also tightens up the casting on. Now hold the cast on portion of the belt around your waist to make sure it is still long enough. If you need to cast on one or two more warps simply untie the knot at the right end and proceed as before.

You are now ready to begin weaving and for this you will need the graphed design. If you read from left to right along the top row of the design below, you will note that the first row of weaving consists of three whites, three blacks, three whites, three blacks, etc., until the end of the row. Keep this sequence in mind as you begin the first row.

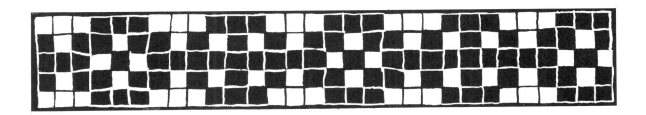

OPPOSITE Enlarged section of taaniko border on a Maori cloak. (Peabody Museum, Salem, Mass.)

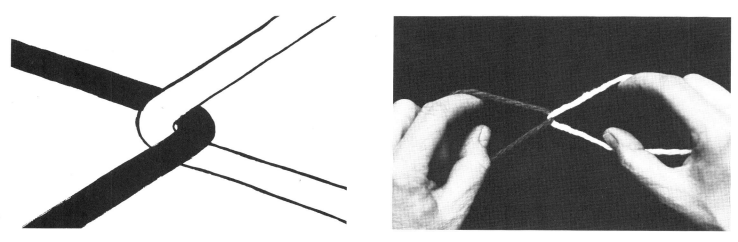

Figure 13   As in casting on, measure one length of each of the two weft colors, *four times* the length of the belt. Hook the two weft fibers together at the mid-point of each one, leaving the two blacks in the left hand and the two whites in the right hand.

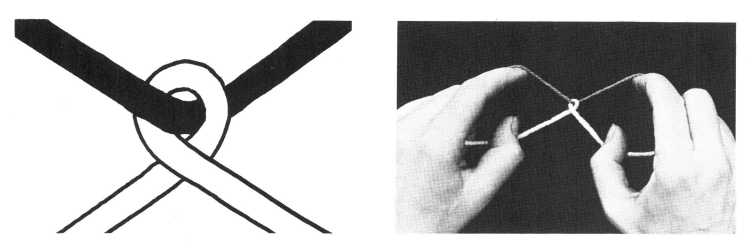

Figure 14   Twist the white weft fibers away from you to make a little loop around the black weft fiber. Now move the black and white pairs so there is one black and one white fiber in the left hand and one black and one white fiber in the right hand.

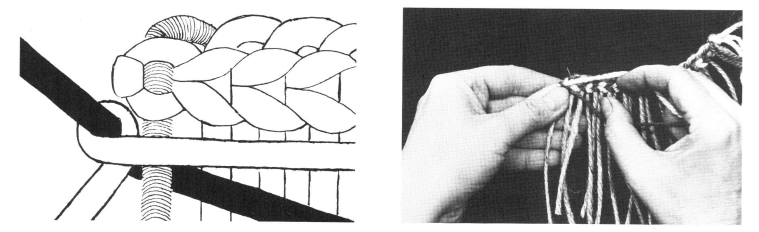

Figure 15   The black and white pair in the left hand will not be used in the first row of weaving but will be saved for the second row. Now place the first warp between the black and white fibers in the right hand, with the white weft on top since your first stitch will be white.

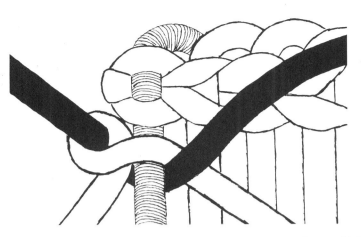

Figure 16 To make the second stitch white, the weft fibers must be twisted *two times* so that the white weft fiber will again be on top. The twisting will not only allow you to alternate the color of your stitches but will also secure each stitch around the warp. (This diagram shows only the first twist, bringing the black weft to the top.)

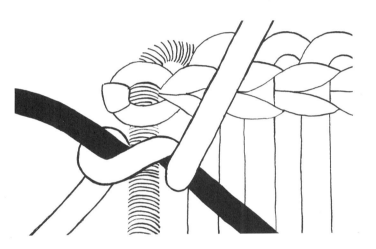

Figure 17 Here you have the second twist, bringing the white weft to the top again.

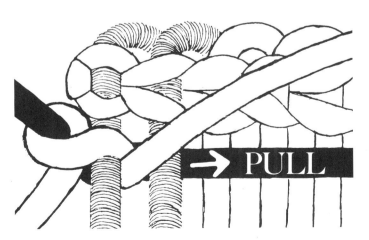

Figure 18 Now place the second warp between the black and white weft fibers. To make sure that the black does not show through between the white stitches, give the black weft fiber a good tug which will pull the stitches closer together.

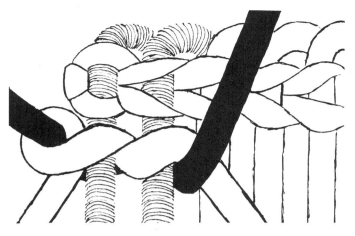

Figure 19   Since the third stitch is also to be white, you must again twist the weft fibers *two times* to bring the white back to the top. Remember that when weaving from left to right, you will always twist away from the body. (This diagram shows only the first twist, bringing the black weft to the top.)

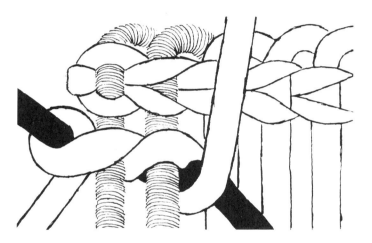

Figure 20   Here you have the second twist, bringing the white weft to the top.

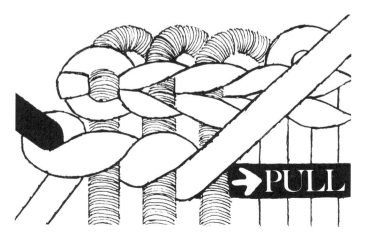

Figure 21   Next place the third warp between the black and white weft fibers with the white on top. Again, to make sure that the black does not show between stitches, give the black weft fiber a good tug, pulling the stitches closer together.

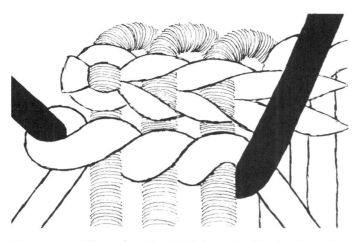

Figure 22 Your fourth stitch is to be black; therefore, you must bring the black weft fiber to the top. This time, as you can see, only *one twist* is necessary. You now have three white stitches encasing the first three warps.

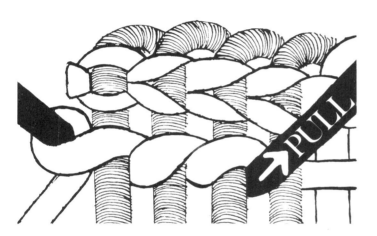

Figure 23 Place the fourth warp between the black and white weft fibers with the black on top. Now pull the top weft fiber, which in this case is black. Remember, when changing the color of stitches, pull the *top* weft fiber, and when repeating the same color, pull the *bottom* weft fiber.

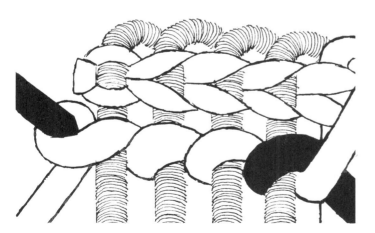

Figure 24 To secure your first black stitch and to begin a second black stitch, twist the weft fibers *two times*. (This diagram shows only the first twist, bringing the white weft to the top.)

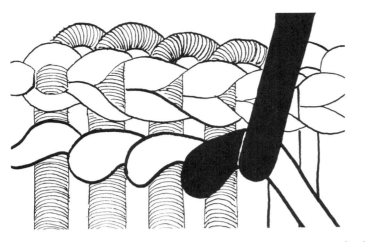 

Figure 25 Here you have the second twist, bringing the black weft to the top.

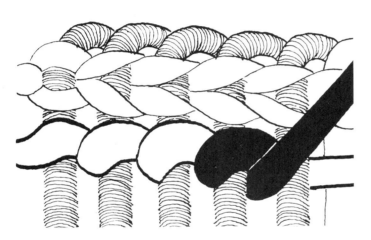 

Figure 26 Now place the fifth warp between the black and white weft fibers with the black on top. To make sure that the white does not show between your black stitches, give the bottom white weft a good tug which will pull the stitches closer together.

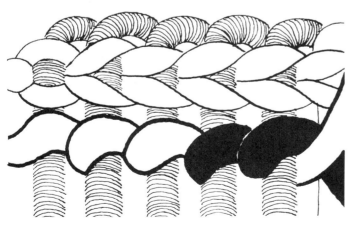 

Figure 27 To begin your third black stitch, twist the weft fibers *two times* to bring the black weft back to the top. (This diagram shows only the first twist, bringing the white weft to the top.)

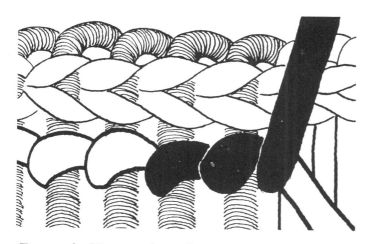

Figure 28 Here you have the second twist, bringing the black weft to the top. You are now ready to encase the next warp with your third black stitch according to your design. Follow your graphed pattern until the end of the row.

The photograph below of a partially completed belt shows a section of the cast on row and the first row of weaving.

At the end of the first row of weaving, tie the weft pair into a square knot. Now go back to the left edge and there will be the other two lengths of black and white weft which will be used in the second row of weaving. As you can see, the weft fibers can be measured to take care of two rows of weaving. (Our design calls for five rows of weaving. In measuring weft for the fifth row, measure *two times* the length of the belt for each color and tie the two in a square knot before beginning weaving.)

CASTING OFF

Soon above, soon below;
Soon to be completed the bottom end . . .

Measure one length of the black fiber *four times* as long as the belt and one length of the white fiber *four times* as long as the belt. These will be the weft fibers used in casting off.

When casting off, the work should be held upside down, with its *back* side facing you and with the warps all pointing up. In the photograph below, you will see that I find placing the work on one knee and pressing down while working the most suitable. Others prefer to press down on a table. At any rate, it seems easier to press onto some surface while casting off rather than holding the work in your hands.

Each weaver will develop slight variations from the above descriptions which only come after doing taaniko awhile. Each weaver also has to discover for himself which precise hand movements are the most comfortable and the most economical for fast weaving.

OPPOSITE. Enlarged section of a Maori cloak covered with tags of rolled strips of flax. (Peabody Museum, Salem, Mass.)

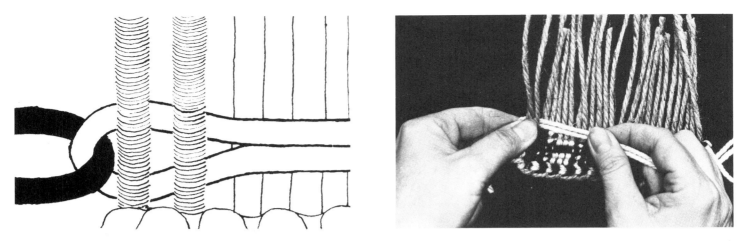

Figure 29   The black and white weft fibers are hooked together at their mid-points. Now hold the weft fibers with the black wefts pointing to the left and the white wefts pointing to the right and place the white wefts in back of the first *two* warps.

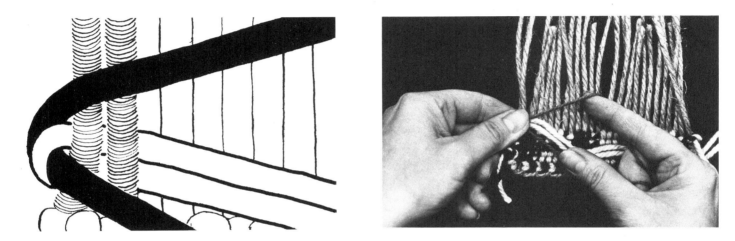

Figure 30   Next spread apart the black weft fibers and bring them over to the right.

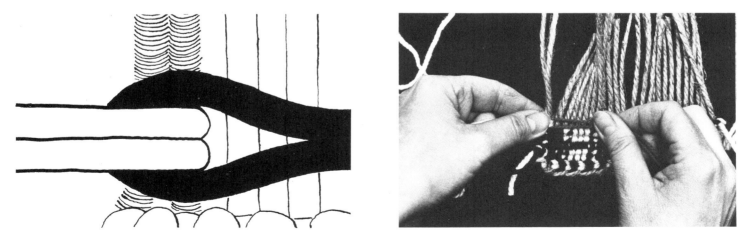

Figure 31   Hold the white weft fibers together and bring them through the black weft fibers and over to the left. Now pull both pair of weft fibers tightly away from each other, which will encase the first two warps.

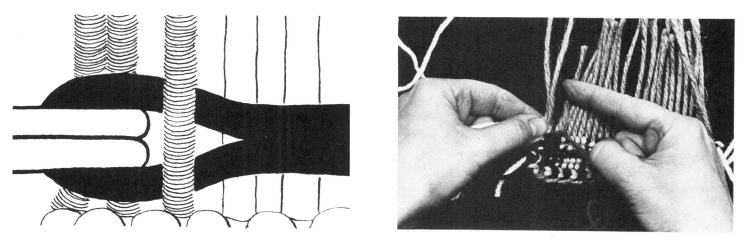

Figure 32   Place the third warp across the black weft fibers as shown.

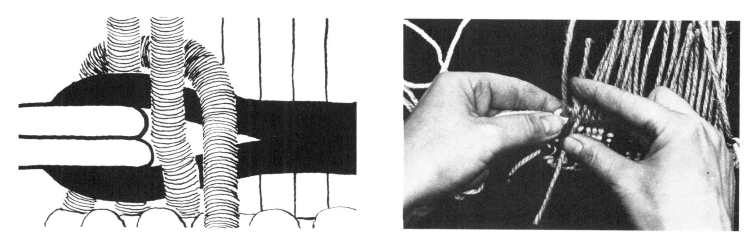

Figure 33   Take the first warp on the *left*, bring it in back of the next two warps and bend it down and on top of the black weft fibers as shown. Pull tightly down with one warp and up with the other.

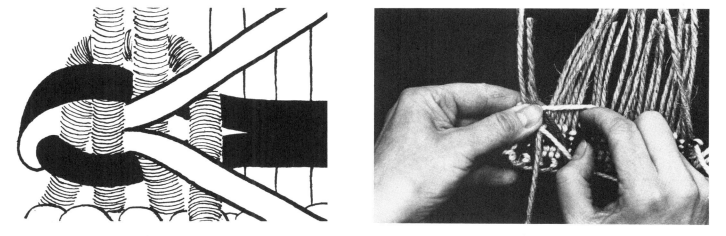

Figure 34   These *two* warps are encased by spreading apart the white weft fibers and bringing them over to the right as shown.

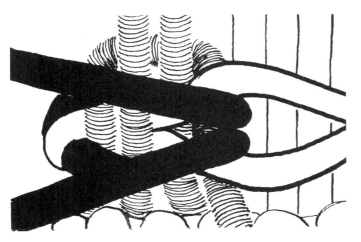 

Figure 35 Now take the black weft fibers through the white weft fibers and over to the left. Pull the wefts in opposing directions, and the first casting off warp enclosure is completed.

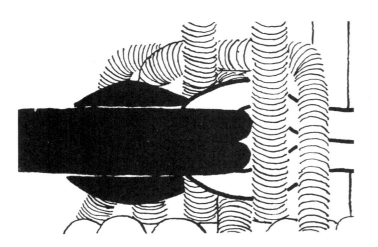 

Figure 36 Continue to secure warps in the same manner, using the two pairs of weft fibers. In casting off it is necessary to work very tightly. When the end of the row is reached, encase the last two warps and tie the two weft pairs into a square knot. Now check the warp loops, and if some need tightening, pull the warp ends until the edge of the belt is firm.

Finishing

Now that the casting on, weaving, and casting off have been completed there is the matter of finishing.

First of all, there will be a row of knots at the right edge of the belt. If there are an uneven number of rows, there will also be one knot at the left edge. Tighten these knots and trim them, leaving the ends one half to one inch long. Bring these ends to the back of the belt and hand stitch them to the underside.

Now turn the belt to the back side and trim off all of the warp ends which have been bent over during the casting off.

After completing each taaniko piece, I always block and steam press it. Using a ruler or any straight edge, draw two parallel lines the width of your belt on an ironing board. Then secure the belt along these lines with pins which will not rust. The belt should be pinned down right side up. Place a damp cloth over the belt and press with a hot iron until the pressing cloth is dry. Then remove the pressing cloth but leave the belt pinned to the ironing board until it is also dry.

The final step is to line the belt to cover the exposed warps on the back side. This can be done with grosgrain ribbon or any lining material. When the belt is lined, a fringe can be added for tying or clasps can be attached, whichever you prefer.

You now have your first taaniko belt.

A series of first project taaniko belts.

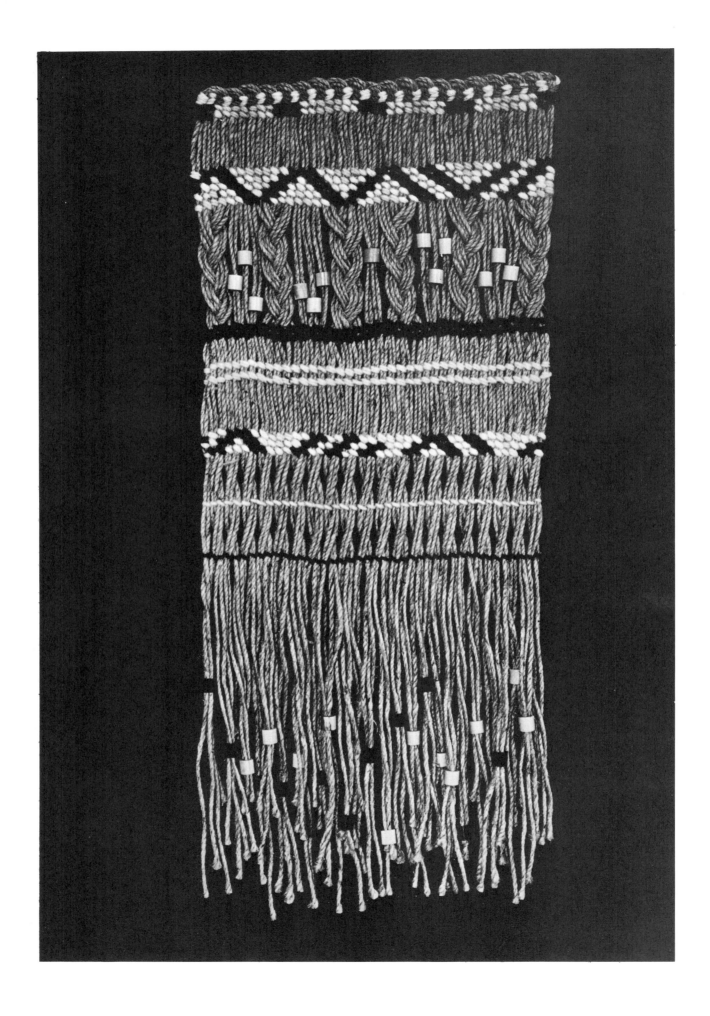

WEAVING VARIATIONS

*. . . there are many possibilities and you will soon be
able to create your own variations.*

In making a taaniko belt all of the basic weaving techniques have been learned. As you have probably discovered, casting off is the most difficult. However, it is only used on belts and headbands. In most cases, hangings, rugs, hand bags, shoulder bags, lamp shades, jewelry, etc., the warps are left hanging down without casting off.

At this point we come to variations on a theme. The Maori developed many variations in the making of cloaks. These have been documented in drawings done by Mead, Roth and Hiroa (Buck) in their books which are listed in the bibliography. In teaching, my students and I have also devised variations. This chapter will present some of the old and some of the new. After trying these, you will realize that there are many possibilities and you will soon be able to create your own variations.

The Sampler

The second project to tackle is what I call a taaniko sampler. As you read about a variation, try it out on the sampler. Try it in different color combinations and different spacings. Then do the same with other variations described.

The result will be a wall hanging which is created as you go along rather than working your design out on graph paper as you did for a belt. The sampler is not only decorative but also will serve as a memory bank to give you ideas for other projects.

The sampler can be any size you want, depending on the size of the warp and weft fibers. It will be best to make it longer than it is wide to give room for experimentation without being crowded as you move down from row to row. If you are using a standard size of jute and rug yarn, a good size for a sampler would be 8 inches wide by 24 inches long.

OPPOSITE Taaniko sampler by Elfrieda Ronald.

Casting On Variations

To begin your sampler the first variation will be to cast on two warps at a time. You could cast on three and four warps at a time but for your first sampler, two will be enough.

Use the jute which you already have for the belt plus one other fiber. This second fiber can be cotton cord, macrame cord, linen, wool, etc. I cannot tell exactly how many warps will be needed to make a sampler 8 inches wide because everyone works with different tension; however, begin by cutting twelve and then cut more as needed. If the sampler is to be 24 inches long, cut the warp lengths to 48 inches. Cut twelve 48-inch strands of the jute and twelve 48-inch strands of the second fiber. Remember that the weft fibers will be *four times* the width of the sampler. Our sampler is to be 8 inches wide; therefore, our weft fibers will be cut 32 inches long.

Cast on in the same manner as for the belt except pick up two warps (one jute length and one length of the second fiber) to encase at a time. It may be awkward to work with such long warps, so try standing up while casting on.

By now you are familiar with the herringbone appearance of casting on. The herringbone will always appear but color variations within that pattern are possible.

The three color variations depend entirely on the way the weft fibers are hooked together before casting on, as illustrated in *Figures 37* through *39*.

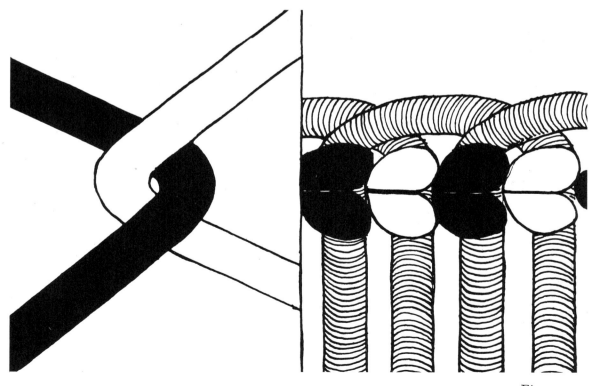

Figure 37

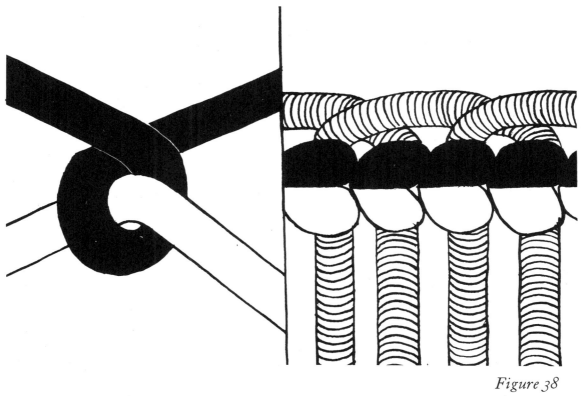

Figure 38

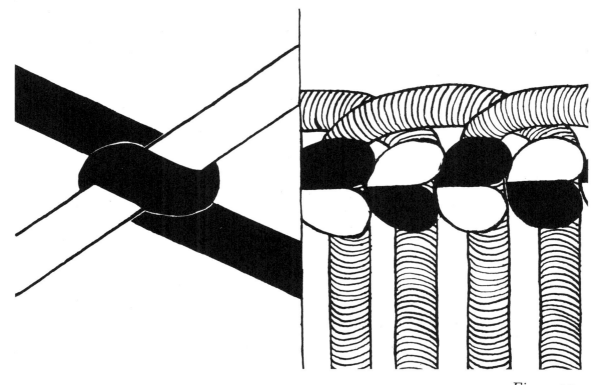

Figure 39

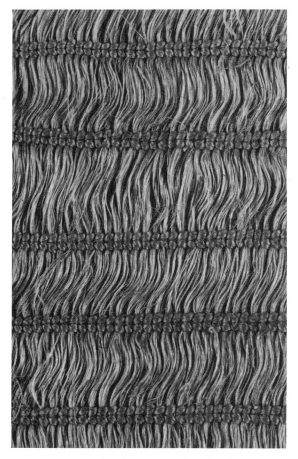

Enlarged kaupapa section of a Maori cloak. (Peabody Museum, Salem, Massachusetts.)

Contemporary kaupapa with heavy homespun fibers.

Kaupapa

The photograph above (left) is an enlarged section of a Maori cloak. The photograph above (right) is an enlarged section of a contemporary purse made with heavy homespun wool. In both photographs the weft rows appear the same as rows of cast on stitches except that here both weft fibers are of one color. The technique of casting on can be used in the body of a piece of weaving as well as at the beginning to secure the warps, and when it is used in such a way it will be referred to as double pair weaving rather than casting on. (For clarity, I will sometimes refer to regular weaving as single pair weaving.)

Also in both photographs you will see a row of double pair weaving followed by a section of exposed warp fibers and then another row of double pair weaving, all the way down the length of the garment. Leaving sections of exposed warp produces a very flexible covering for the body and this is how the Maori made the main section of their cloaks, referred to as the kaupapa section.

The kaupapa method of exposing warp fibers can lead to all kinds of experimentation. For example, the exposed warps can be crossed or braided; beads, feathers and other materials can be attached to the warps; the rows of double or single pair weaving can encase two or more warps at a time.

Enlarged sections of taaniko samplers showing some of the variations possible in braiding and crossing exposed warps.

Other Variations

Using more than two colors – When three or more colors are to be used the weaving is done basically the same way. As you twist to bring to the top the desired color for the next stitch, carry the other colors on the bottom together as one fiber. When you wish to change colors simply bring up to the top the color desired and carry the others on the bottom. It is no more difficult than weaving with two colors although it will produce a thicker and heavier piece of weaving.

Top pull – When repeating the same color, two twists are required followed by pulling hard on the bottom fiber. If you do the same thing but pull hard on the *top* fiber, a little bead of the underneath color will appear between the two stitches. This can be seen in the photograph below. (The two horizontal rows of weaving in the center of the picture make use of top pull weaving.)

Weaving a large area of one color – If you are weaving something which requires large areas of one color interspaced with patterns of color, you can use the same color for both weft fibers. For example, if you have a large area of white to weave closely together, no kaupapa, you can use two lengths of white fibers for the single pair weaving. However, even though both weft fibers are of the same color, you must still twist *two times*, for if you weave a large area by only twisting once, the stitches will be slightly smaller and this part of your sampler (or whatever you may be working on) will be narrower than the rest. (An occasional single twist can be used within a row without significantly changing the shape of your work.)

Weaving back and forth in single pair weaving – Start by weaving from the left to the right in the usual way. When you get to the end of the row, twist the fibers two or three times, depending on which color is to show on the beginning of the next row on the right-hand end.

Now you are ready to start weaving from right to left. Follow the same rules by twisting two times to repeat a color; however, *twist now with your left hand*, not the right, and *twist toward your body* rather than away from it. Pull on the bottom weft fiber after twisting two times. To change color, just as before, twist one time, but now with the left hand and twist toward your body.

Basically the same rules hold true – just use your left hand and twist toward you. After doing this for several rows, you will be ambidextrous and weaving in both directions will seem easy.

When weaving back and forth, plan to have the two strands of the single pair, of different lengths. Then when one color runs out, knot on another length and make certain that the knot falls to the back of the piece of weaving. This way the knots will be at random on the back side rather than on the right edge.

Weaving back and forth will make finishing much easier, for if you weave from left to right, and then again from left to right, etc., the right edge will be filled with knots. All of these knots will have to be trimmed and the ends worked back into the weaving with a crochet hook. However, in weaving back and forth, none of this will be necessary and both edges will be smooth and even.

Weaving around multiple warps – In the photograph below you can see that the single pair weaving starts out by encasing two warps at a time and ends up encasing ten warps at a time. The more warps that are encased by the weaving, the larger the open spaces become. When weaving around multiple warps you will find that it is necessary to twist the weft pair of fibers more than the usual two times between stitches. This will produce the required stiffness to separate the multiple warps encased by a single weaving stitch. (At the bottom of this hanging, ten twists were made between stitches. Also in this hanging, you will notice examples of weaving with more than two colors, top pull weaving and double pair weaving.)

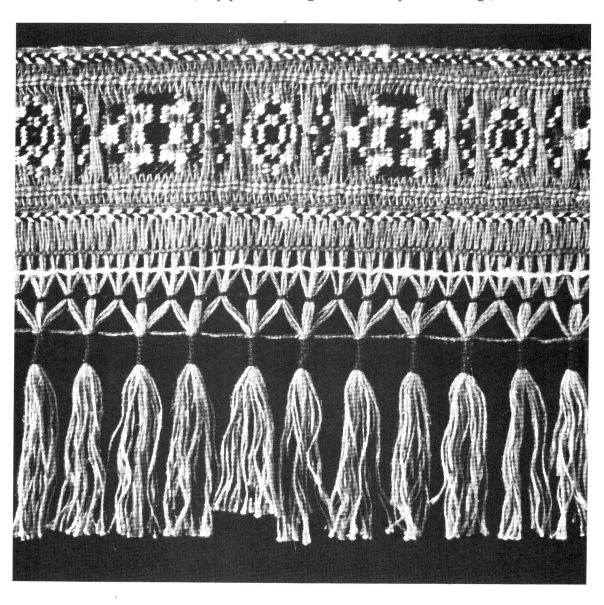

Contrast in weight between warps and weft – In the photograph below a very heavy homespun alpaca is used as a warp while a fine linen and polished cotton is used as weft. Note the contrasting patterns and textures between warps and weft.

Weaving three-dimensionally – When weaving a hand bag or shoulder bag simply cast on a length twice as long as the intended width of the bag, and then attach the two ends to form a circle. Now start weaving continuously around and around for as long as you want the bag to be and you will have eliminated side seams. The only seam will be on the bottom. This circular method of weaving can also be used for lamp shades.

Finishing the warp ends when not casting off – Casting off at the end of a hanging or rug sometimes makes the bottom edge too bulky and is not really necessary. The last row of weaving, whether single pair or double pair, will be firm enough to end the work. There is no need to worry; the weft rows will not slip down on the warp.

The photograph below shows a simple ending. Double pair weaving was used in the last row for reasons of design rather than for any structural reason.

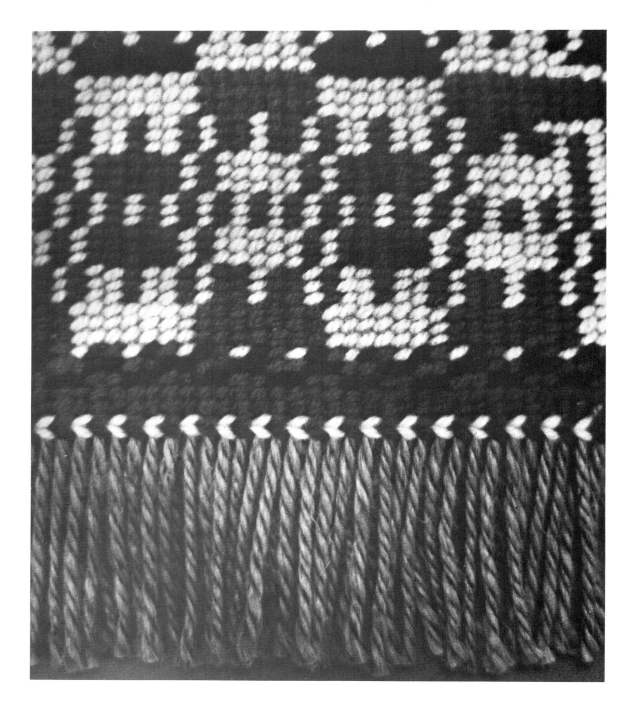

Sometimes wrapping the warp ends or groups of warp ends can be visually effective, as shown in the photograph below.

Begin by measuring the fiber that is to do the wrapping at least ten times longer than the length of warp to be wrapped. Then proceed as shown in *Figure 40a* by placing the end of the wrapping fiber about an inch above the free end of the warp. Then run the wrapping fiber down the side of the warp and around the bottom as shown in *Figure 40b*. Continue wrapping up the length of the warp toward the body of weaving as shown in *Figure 40c*. When you have reached the bottom row of weaving, the end of the wrapping fiber can be tucked into the back side of the weaving with a crochet hook.

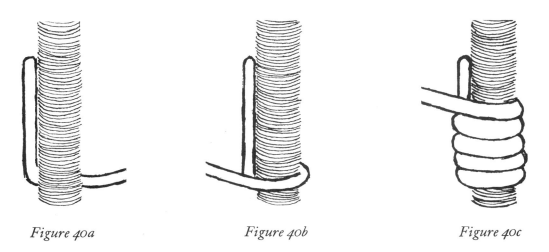

Figure 40a   *Figure 40b*   *Figure 40c*

Figures 41 through *44* are adaptations of drawings which appear in S.M. Mead's book *Traditional Maori Clothing* and Te Rangi Hiroa's book *The Evolution of Maori Clothing*.

Mead's and Hiroa's books, which are listed in the bibliography, contain many other fascinating Maori variations.

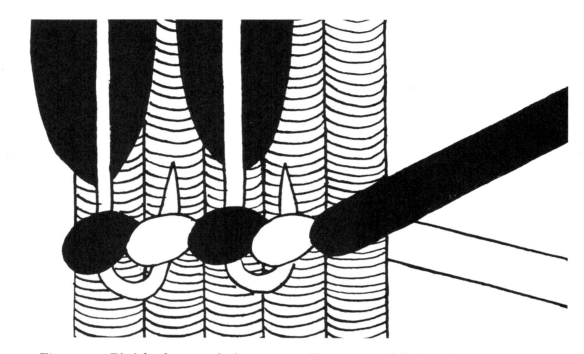

Figure 41   Bird feathers can be incorporated into a row of single pair weaving.

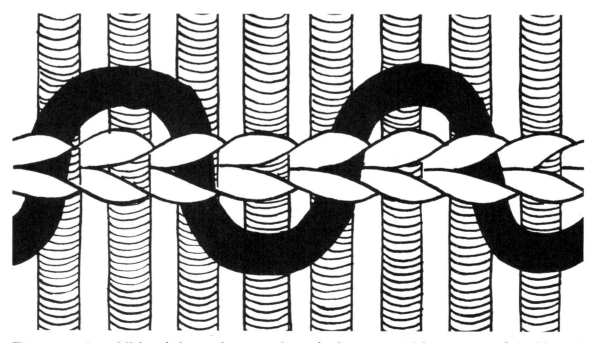

Figure 42   An additional decorative strand can be incorporated into a row of double pair weaving.

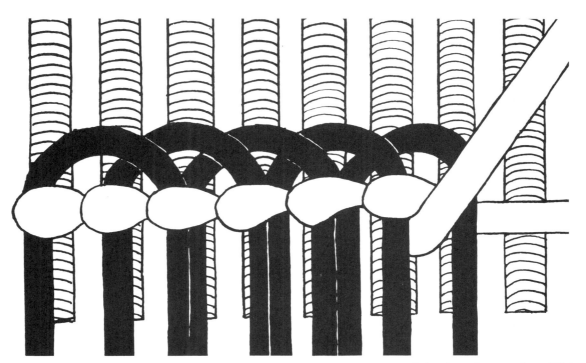

Figure 43 An extra layer of warps can be added within a row of single pair weaving. This extra layer can hang decoratively or can be woven with. This method of adding warps is a completely unexplored technique and my students have found it very useful in making jewelry, lamp shades and other three-dimensional projects.

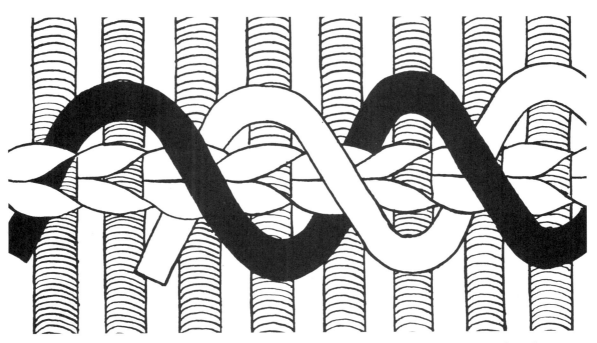

Figure 44 This variation is similar to that illustrated in *Figure 42* except that here *two* strands are incorporated into a row of double pair weaving.

APPLICATIONS

Heaped up to the sky,
Widely across the land.

After working on a taaniko sampler you should now be at ease weaving back and forth, using more than two colors, top pull weaving, kaupapa warp spacing, double pair weaving and all of the other weaving variations described in Chapter V.

At this point each person branches out in a different direction. Some want to make hand bags or shoulder bags, others want to concentrate on experimental hangings and still others prefer to weave rugs or mats, experiment with three-dimensional projects or try their hand at jewelry.

The photographs on the following pages illustrate the variety of projects and effects that can be achieved with taaniko weaving.

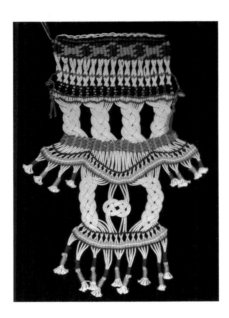

OPPOSITE Enlarged section of a Maori cloak covered with rolled strips of flax. (Peabody Museum, Salem, Mass.)

Wall hanging by Karen Seprish.

OPPOSITE Enlarged section of a wall hanging by Alice Rock.

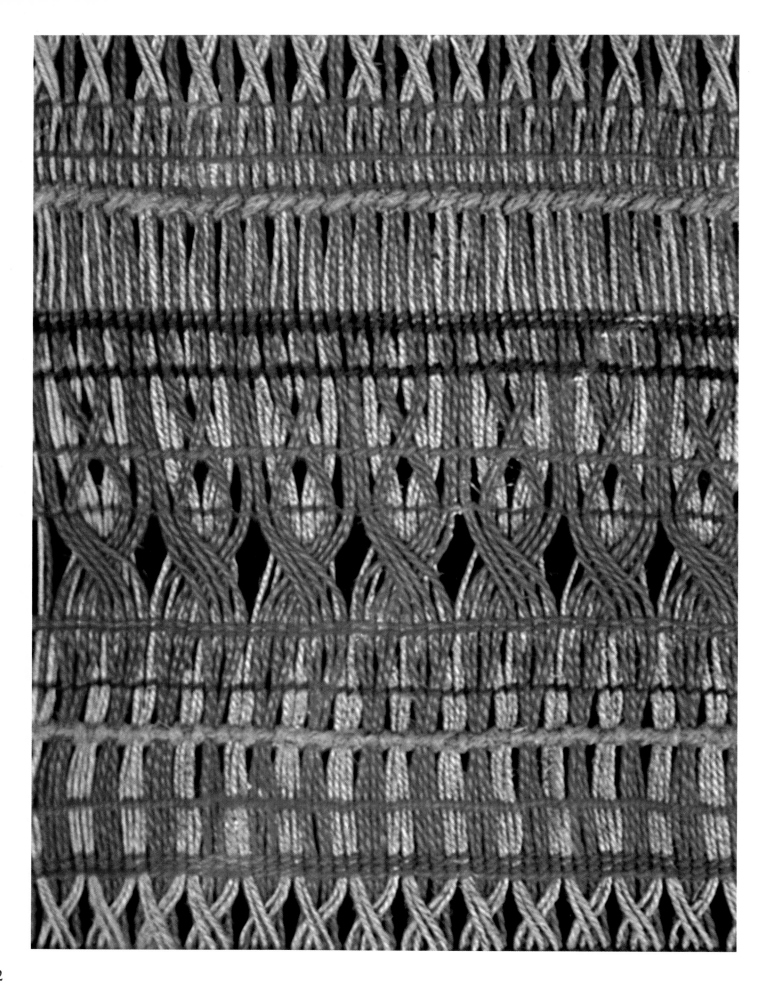

Taaniko necklace by author.

OPPOSITE Enlarged section of a wall hanging by Barbara Surprenant.

73

Hand bag by author.

OPPOSITE Taaniko rug by author from the collection of Judge and Mrs. James Bandy.

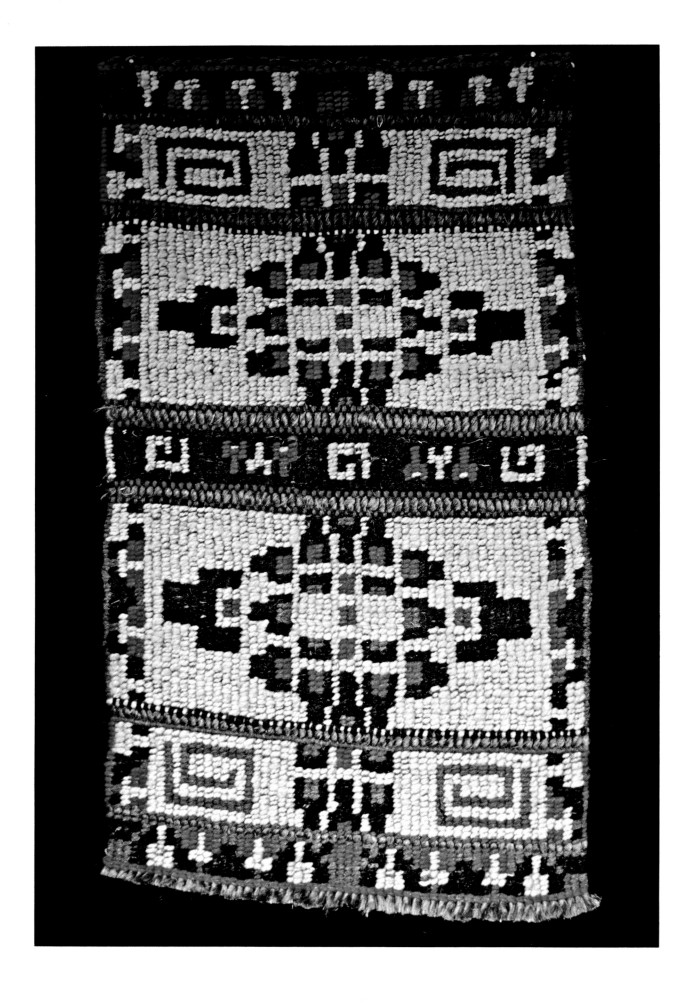

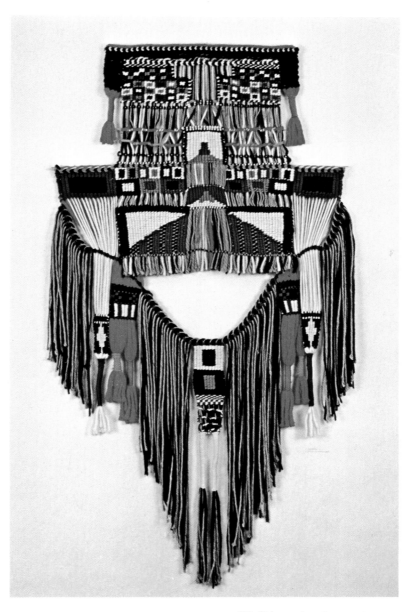

Wall hanging by author.

OPPOSITE Taaniko rug by author.

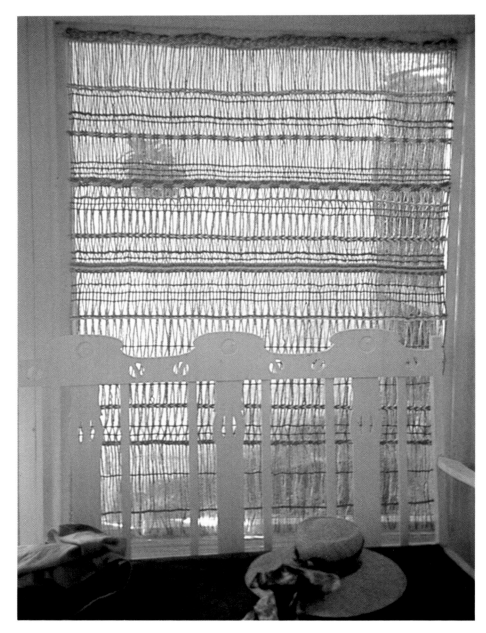

Window covering at our cottage in Russell. Here you can see maximum use of warp exposure.

OPPOSITE Taaniko rug by author.

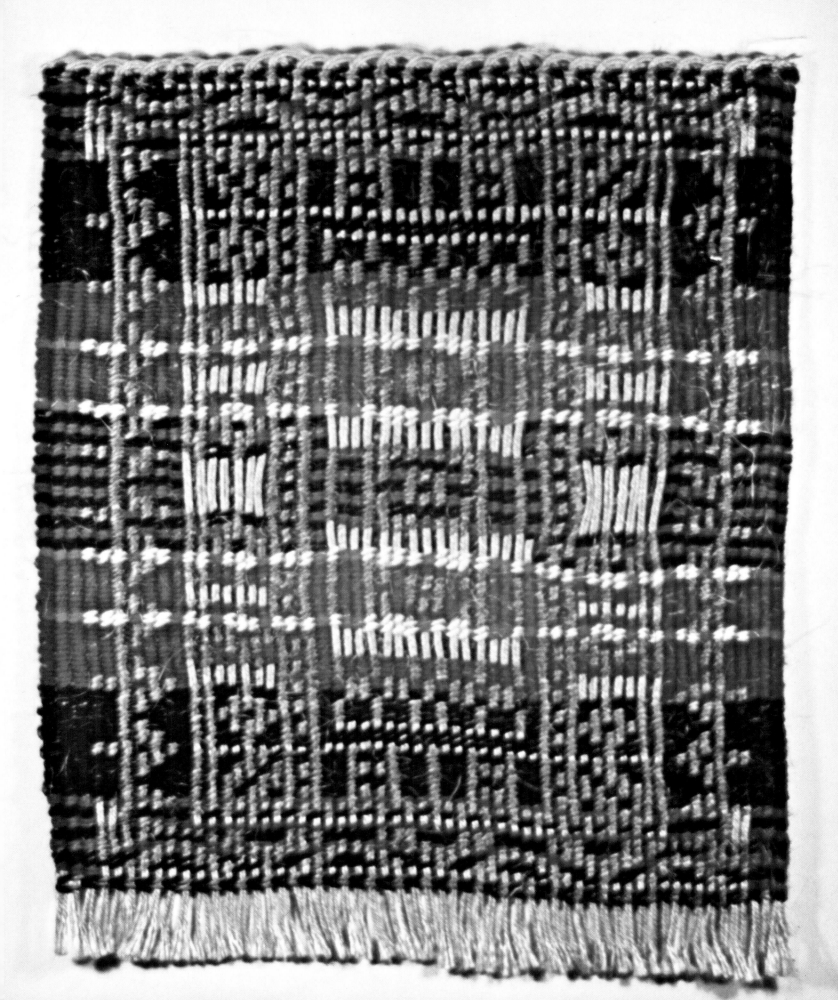

Enlarged section of the wall hanging on opposite page.

OPPOSITE Wall hanging by author from the collection of Hugo Leckey.

Enlarged section of the wall hanging on opposite page.

OPPOSITE "Miss Kitty" by Nancy Hamilton from the collection of Margaret Lewis and Clara Taylor.

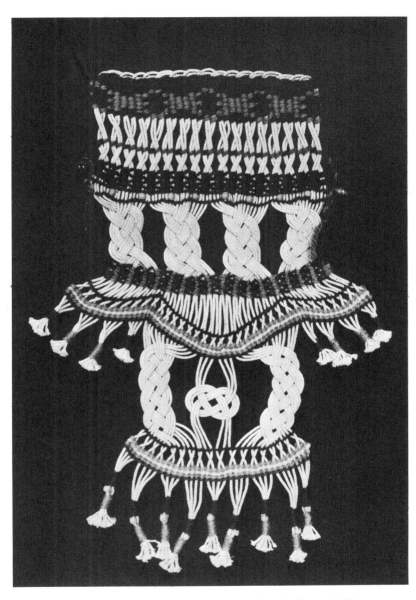

Taaniko sampler by Lynda Emerson.

OPPOSITE Enlarged section of a wall hanging by the author.

Turn your face to the sun and the shadows will fall behind you.

Maori proverb

OPPOSITE Enlarged section of a Maori cloak covered with Kiwi feathers. (Peabody Museum, Salem, Mass.)

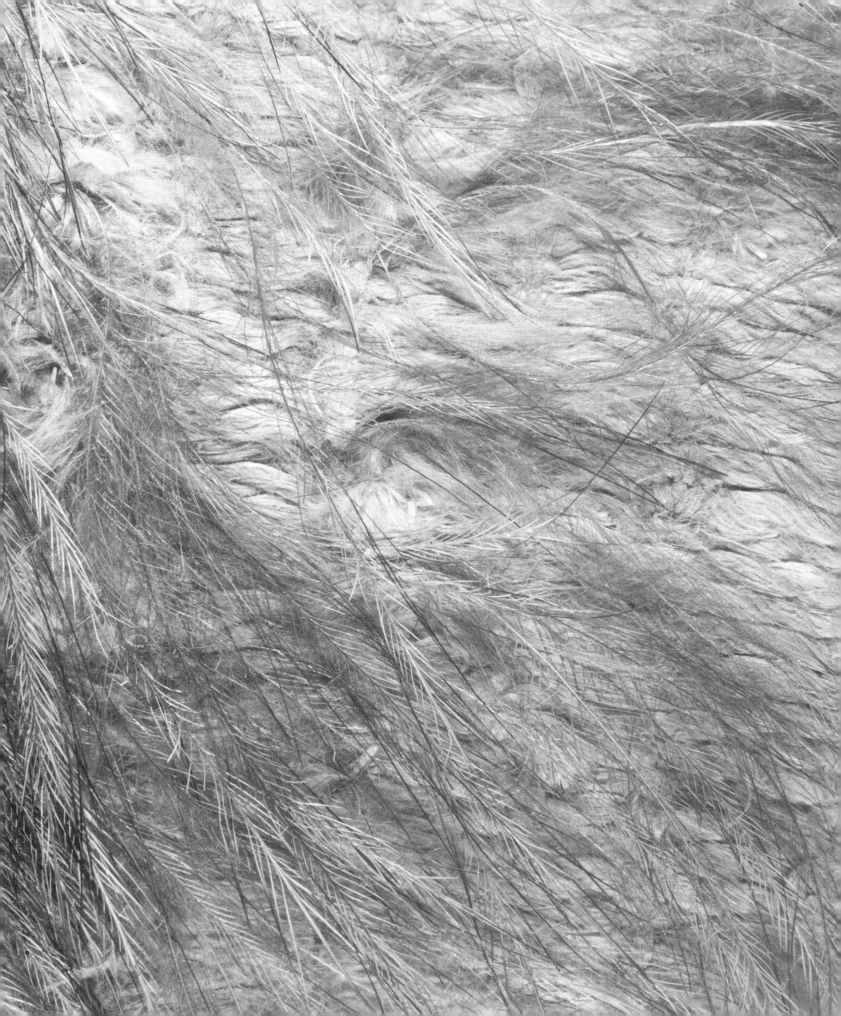

Appendix I

PREPARING THE FLAX FOR WEAVING

The following is taken from S.M. Mead's book *The Art of Taaniko Weaving*:

The first step in the preparation of weaving elements is to cut from a superior variety [flax] such as the oue, unmarked leaves from one year to 18 months old. The outer decaying leaves of the plant known as pakawhaa were cut and discarded to allow other leaves a chance to grow freely. . . . When a bundle of muka (fibre) leaves had been collected it was carried home by the weaver. Near the safety and comfort of her home she would begin the slow task of stripping each blade and extracting the white fibre. From each complete leaf the edges and midrib were removed and the fibre was extracted by one of two methods, or a combination of both.

1. The haaro method: A light cut is made across the underside of a strand of flax about halfway along its length. The flax strand is held securely by the left hand immediately behind the cut. A mussel shell held in the right hand is placed over the top surface of the flax strand opposite the cut. Then slowly the shell is dragged over the blade in an outward motion for about 5 inches. This action causes the underside to separate. To facilitate the easy removal of the fibre from this point, a loop is made in the underpart and then with one final sweep of the right hand the waste material from the blade is stripped off. . . . After this, the blade of flax is turned around and the process is repeated on the other half. . . .

When a sufficient quantity of fibres was so prepared they were given a final scraping and a thorough washing. Beating with a wooden or stone pounder upon a rounded well-worn river stone followed.

2. The takiri method: This method of removing fibre is used most successfully only with certain kinds of flax. A cut is made on the underside, as before, and then the flax blade is folded over so that the cut opens out. While the folded piece is held in the left hand the top half is grasped in the right hand. The top half is pressed firmly down against the left hand, while at the same time it is drawn away from the area of the cut. This action causes the lower portion of the flax to separate from the upper. When the weaver sees that the separation has begun smoothly, her two hands jerk suddenly away from each other, continuing the action until separation is complete. . . .

After being thoroughly scraped [using either method] the fibre is washed and then scraped again to make the fibres absolutely clean and white. Then they are dried . . . and separated into hanks. . . . Many cloaks were [made] of fibre prepared only to this stage. However, if a softer fibre is required, then they are washed again. The treatment is followed by a period of beating with stone pounders on flat water-worn stones. . . . Then the fibres are washed, dried and hanked. . . .

Rolling the fibres into cords. . . . The Maori method . . . is not unique; other primitive societies, namely some in New Guinea and New Britain, employ a similar technique. However, there are some points of detail which are probably peculiar to the Maori.

The thickness of the cords depends on how many individual fibres are rolled together, so it is important to work this out beforehand. For warp threads a usual number is 18 to 20, and for weft threads about 10. . . .

The total number of individual fibres are halved, two lots of five for weft and two lots of nine for the thicker warp threads. These halved sections have one end held in the left hand while the other end is placed over the right leg just above the knee. The two sections are 2 inches apart. Then the fingers of the free right hand are placed over the fibres and pressure is applied against the skin of the thigh. Pushing gently against the skin and at the same time using the left hand to keep some tension on the two lots of fibre, the weaver now pushes her hand forward away from her body. As she does so, the fibres begin to roll under her fingers, then under the palm of her hand and finally past the wrist and along the arm. By this time the fibres are down the leg below the knee.

The return movement from below the knee to the starting position now fuses the two halves into a thread consisting of two parts. . . .

Extra lengths are added to the thread by simply rolling them in with the appropriate series of rolling movements. . . .

Appendix II

HOW THE FIBERS WERE DYED

The following is taken from S.M. Mead's book *The Art of Taaniko Weaving* (Best and Buck that Mead refers to are Elsdon Best and Sir Peter Henry Buck respectively):

How the fibres were dyed: The patterns of taaniko borders in cloaks such as the kaitaka and paepaeroa were worked by varying the colours brought forward to cover each warp. In very old work there was more black used than any other colour, and even now black remains the dominant colour, although there is less of it used. Various colours were used in conjunction with black; some yellow, red, and some natural fibre representing white.

We shall deal with the methods used by the Maori for producing these colours. Part of the information supplied here has been gained from informants through questioning and discussions, and part from the works of Best and Buck.

1. The yellow dye: A yellow dye was obtained from the coprosma tree, usually the karamu. My informants claimed that a richer yellow was obtained from the kanono tree (*Coprosma australis*) which in the pioneer days provided the "bushmen's iodine". When the roots were cooked they became soft and the juice could be extracted easily from the root. It was this juice which was used as a dye, or in lieu of iodine for treating any open wounds or cuts. My informants recalled using kanono juice for tanning leather. For this purpose it was more effective than taanekaha (*Phyllocladus*), but my informants were a little confused over whether the resulting colour was more yellow than red or vice versa. . . .

2. The red dye: According to my informants, a red-brown, described as being a little redder than the colour of varnish, was obtained by soaking the fibres in an infusion of taanekaha. Apparently Maori farmers of the East Coast used to tan their animal hides in this same mixture leaving each hide in the dye bath for two nights before drying. Best describes how the mixture was prepared: the bark was pounded and then boiled in a wooden bowl (kumete). Heated stones were placed in the bowl and when the mixture boiled the prepared fibres were put into it and left there to soak. The fibres were then taken out of the mixture and rolled in hot clean ashes or powdered charcoal, after which they were soaked in the taanekaha mixture again.

We are told by Barrow that a deeper colour resulted from the use of the burnt and powdered bark of the toatoa (*Phyllocladus tricomanoides*) but it is not explained how the powdered bark was used. He adds that a golden-brown was obtained by using the bark of a large-leaved karamu-rau-nui (*Coprosma robusta*) instead of taanekaha, in which case rolling in ashes to fix the colour was not necessary.

3. The black dye: Obtaining a suitable and fast black was a much more complex process than those described so far, and it appears to be the only one which involved some prohibitions on the part of the weaver. A mordant (waitumu) of either makomako (*Aristotelia serrata*) whiinau (*Elaeocarpus dentatus*), or tutu (*Coriaria arborea*) was prepared by pounding the bark upon a flat stone. This crushed bark was mixed with cold water in a wooden bowl. The [flax] was immersed in this mixture and left to soak for 12 hours, after which it was hung up to dry. My informant maintained that if the makomako mordant was used, the flax was best left to soak for two nights.

After the flax is soaked in one of the mordants mentioned it is then taken to be dipped into a special black mud. The mud, known as maramara to Buck and as uku to my informants, is rusty coloured on top and is usually to be found in swamps. Some weavers pour a portion of the mordant into the mud and this is then stirred, but this action is really unnecessary. The rust now disappears and the mud changes to a deep black colour and after thorough agitation is ready to be used as a dye. The flax fibre, which has been first treated in the mordant so that it will take a permanent colour, is now dipped into the mud and the strands are manipulated with the hands to ensure that all parts are in contact with it. As each bundle was so handled, it was left in the mud while other bundles were dipped in. Much care and patience were needed for this work.

My informants went on to say that when a patch of mud is used for dyeing purposes for the first time it is usual to immerse the first lot of flax for two nights. Thereafter, one night is sufficient. Buck gave 8 to 10 hours as the required time. . . .

After the flax is pulled out of the mud it is washed thoroughly in running water and then dried out in the shade. If the correct procedures have been followed, the flax fibres should be a deep permanent black.

Glossary

Bark cloth — the bark of the Asiatic paper mulberry tree, used by the Polynesians to make a kind of cloth sometimes referred to as tapa cloth.

Calabash — vessel made from the shell of a gourd from the calabash tree.

Casting off — in taaniko, a method of folding back exposed warp ends.

Casting on — in taaniko, a method of joining warps to begin a piece of weaving.

Double pair weaving — in taaniko, weaving with two pairs of weft fibers.

Gusset — a small triangular piece of cloth fitted into a garment to give added strength or more room.

Haaro — a method of preparing flax for weaving in which the flax fiber is removed from the leaves by cutting across the underside of the leaves and is then drawn across a shell.

Kaakahu roimata — a cloak made for burial purposes, referred to as the cloak of tears.

Kaitaka — a class of cloaks worn by the Maori that are decorated with taaniko borders.

Kaupapa — the body of a cloak that is more loosely woven than the taaniko borders and which is woven using warp spacing.

Kumete — a wooden bowl into which hot stones are placed to boil water.

Kummera — a potato similar to the American sweet potato only more nutty in flavor, used as a main part of the Maori diet.

Maori — the original Polynesian inhabitants of New Zealand.

Maramara — a term for mud used in obtaining a black dye.

Mordant — a substance which, combined with a dyestuff, produces a fixed color in a textile fiber.

Muka — fibers.

Oue — a superior variety of flax.

Pa — a Maori fortified village.

Paepaeroa — a cloak with vertical wefts in the body and double taaniko borders along the side and bottom.

Pakawhaa — outside dried leaves of a flax plant.

Pakeha — indigenous white turnip. Now popularly used to describe a white man whose skin resembles that of a turnip.

Polynesia — the islands of Oceania lying east of Melanesia and Micronesia extending from the Hawaiian Islands to New Zealand.

Phormium tenax — native flax plant of New Zealand.

Single pair weaving — in taaniko, weaving with one pair of fibers.

Taawhiu — in taaniko, the first weft thread which is stretched between the two weaving pegs.

Tags — bits or strands of fiber or hair that are incorporated into the weaving of a cloak.

Takiri — jerking method used to strip fiber away from the flax leaves.

Tohunga — a priest.

Top pull — a weaving variation in taaniko.

Turu-turu — weaving pegs, the right one of which is sacred.

Waitumu — a mordant used in dying flax.

Warp — in weaving, the fibers which run vertically.

Weft — in weaving, the fibers which run horizontally.

Whare para — weaving guild.

Whare tauaa — the house of mourning.

What tangi — the weaving of lamentation involving the making of a cloak for the dead.

Bibliography

Barrow, Terence. "Taniko Weaving of the New Zealand Maori," *Pallette*, IX (Spring 1962).

Best, Elsdon. *The Maori As He Was*. Wellington: Dominion Museum, 1924.

————. "The Art of the Whare Pora," *Transactions of the New Zealand Institute*, Volume XXXI (1898).

————. *The Maori*. Wellington: Memoir of Polynesian Society, Volumes I and II, 1941.

Buck, Sir Peter Henry (Te Rangi Hiroa). *The Evolution of Maori Clothing*. Wellington: Memoir of Polynesian Society, 1926.

————. *The Coming of the Maori*. Wellington: Whitcombe & Tombs, 1949.

Jackson, Keith and Harre, John. *New Zealand*. New York: Walker & Co., 1969.

Mead, S.M. *The Art of Maori Carving*. Wellington: A.H. & A.W. Reed, 1961.

————. *The Art of Taaniko Weaving*. Wellington: A.H. & A.W. Reed, 1968.

————. *Traditional Maori Clothing*. Wellington: A.H. & A.W. Reed, 1969.

Richardson, Elwyn S. *In the Early World*. New York: Random House, 1964.

Roth, Henry Ling. *The Maori Mantle*. Halifax: Bankfield Museum, 1923.

Rout, Ettie A. *Maori Symbolism*. London: Harcourt, Brace & Co., 1926.

Index